HOME OFFICE + PRODUCTIVE

21 TIPS TO IMPROVE YOUR RESULTS

Lilian Aveiro

Copyright © 2021 Lilian Aveiro

All rights reserved

The author has endeavored to be as accurate and complete as possible in the creation of this book, in any case she does not guarantee at any time the content described due to the rapid changes that exist on the internet.

Although every attempt has been made to verify all information in this publication, the editor assumes no responsibility for errors, omissions or misinterpretations of this book. Any references to specific people or organizations are not intentional.

In practical advice books, as in life, there are no guarantees for an income. Readers must make their own judgment about their circumstances and act accordingly.

This book is not intended to be used as a legal advisor. All readers are advised to seek the services of competent professionals in the legal fields.

No part of this book may be reproduced or stored in a retrieval system, or transmitted in any form or by any means, electronic, mechanical, photocopying, recording or otherwise, without express permission.

ISBN-13 : 979-8594141162
ASIN: BO8L5KK6NH and B08SXWPWTW

Editorial Stamp - Independently Published

Cover design by: LILIAN AVEIRO

I dedicate this book to my parents Lino and Dina, my husband Antonio and my son Caio.

Without your support, it would not be possible to get here.

Thank you my loves!

Thank you!

"When written in Chinese the word 'crisis' is composed of two characters – one represents danger and the other represents opportunity."

JOHN F. KENNEDY

CONTENTS

Title Page
Copyright
Dedication
Epigraph
Introduction   1
Tip - 1   5
Tip - 2   11
Tip - 3   15
Tip - 4   19
Tip - 5   23
Tip - 6   29
Tip - 7   33
Tip - 8   37
Tip - 9   41
Tip - 10   45
Tip - 11   49
Tip - 12   53
Tip - 13   59
Tip - 14   63
Tip - 15   67
Tip - 16   71

Tip - 17	77
Tip - 18	81
Tip - 19	85
Tip - 20	89
Tip - 21	93
About The Author	99
Books By This Author	101

INTRODUCTION

If you are working from home, your capability to perform many tasks will have a huge impact on your lifestyle and happiness. Quit early and you have the option to simply go down the stairs, make a cup of coffee and start relaxing!

There is no commuting, boss looking over his shoulder and no need to work at fixed times (as long as the job is done). Of course, you can also take advantage of that extra time by starting a side project, further developing your skills, etc.

Then there is the fact that working from home can mean working in your perfect work environment, close to the people you love and with the freedom to come and go as you want, or even completely change your working hours!

But if you don't have the discipline and motivation to actually get the job done, it can be a completely different story. Now you are more likely to find the experience highly stressful and overwhelming: you may find yourself with a huge list of tasks that you have no idea how to handle. The line between downtime and work may have been blurred, and you may be constantly working late, forgetting to shave or take care of yourself, and generally cannot maintain a work-life balance.

Keep reading and you will discover 21 productivity tips, which can make a huge difference!

TIP -1

Home Office In Practice

Some people claim that the main reason they seek to work from home is because they can only produce when they want to work. It is true that you can determine your own working hours when you are at home, but that does not mean that you do not need to set working hours.

Working from home can be a very, very good thing. You can see the kids go to school and it will be there when they get back. While you work, you can put the washing machine to work and prepare dinner before a hungry family arrives.

These are real benefits that you automatically get when you work from home. However, working from home can be quite complicated, if you don't plan your time well and don't set a work schedule that you and your family can live with. When you work from home, time is really essential.

It is important to make good use of the time you spend working. If you are not efficient in accomplishing the tasks that must be performed, you will spend too much time working or fail at your tasks, at work or in business.

You must set a work schedule for yourself when you work from home and you must enforce that schedule and insist that your family and friends also stick to your work schedule.

First, analyze the structure that a regular job provides and how you can apply it to your work at home. When you have a job for which you work in the company structure, you must have a set time on specific days of the week.

When you work from home, you need that same type of structure. You need to set the regular working hours. The freedom that a work at home provides is that you can choose the hours ... But you have to choose!

Now reflect on your family and friends and how they will see your work at home. It is a strange but very common fact that your dear mom would not dream of calling you in her "real" job, the one in the office and asking you to take Aunt Mary to the supermarket and wait for her ... Correct?

But when you're working from home, that same kind mom will call you and ask you to take Aunt Mary to the supermarket and wait for her ... Why? Because you are at home and "free", that's why. These things can happen ... So you need to make it clear that you are working, so you cannot be expected to interrupt your work to do favors.

Your dear mom will not see your work at home as a "real"

job. Your spouse will also see you as free to do favors. Your friends will see you as available for long phone conversations, lunch or coffee.

Can you understand the problem? If you don't organize your schedule and stick to your schedule, others won't help. Unless you see your work at home as a REAL job with a REAL work schedule, your time will be consumed by several interruptions and you will not be doing the tasks you need.

You will fail and find yourself looking for a REAL job, unless you see your work at home as REAL with regular hours that make you unavailable for other activities.

The best way to enjoy your time at the home office is to make a schedule and tell your family and friends what that schedule is.

You don't have to be rude, but you do need to be firm. Make it clear to everyone. "I will work between 9 am and 3 pm, Monday to Friday. These days and during these hours, I am not available to do favors and receive personal phone calls."

The most important of all is to practice, to maintain limits.

TIP - 2

Eat The Frog

Eating the frog is an expression that comes from a quote by Mark Twain: "If it's your job to eat a frog, it's best to do it first thing in the morning. And if it's your job to eat two frogs, it's best to eat the biggest one first".

Looking at your to-do list for the day, you are likely to go to the tasks that are easiest, those that do not require much effort. This is procrastination causing you to postpone the most difficult and often most important tasks until later.

However, it is noticed in many cases, that your day is optimized when the most difficult and or painful tasks occur at the beginning of the day. The reasoning is simple: we feel good when an experience gets better over time, not worse. If this is the way your days go, in general, you will remember it as a good day, which will make you happier.

When starting your regular workday, review your list of tasks and identify the ones you don't like and tend to procrastinate. Then start your day with these tasks. Soon they will be finished and out of the way and your day will start to improve immediately afterwards.

The same principle applies to long-term projects or even starting your own business. So, start with the heaviest work, this will help you fight the postponement and you will be closer to reaching your goals.

What this tells us is that it is wise to tackle the biggest and most difficult project first. In doing so, be sure to provide the maximum value each day and do the hardest work while you have the most energy and determination.

TIP - 3

Kaizen

Kaizen is a Japanese term that means "improvement" or "change for the better" from the country's manufacturing industry.

"Today better than yesterday, tomorrow better than today!"

For this method, it is always possible to do better, any day should pass without any improvement having been implemented, be it in the structure of the company or in the individual.

The Kaizen refers to minor changes to process in a process in order to obtain a large cumulative benefit over time.

For example, if your computer currently takes 5 minutes to start up and you start it twice a day, it means that you are losing 10 minutes of productive time daily. So it would be better to use that time to do something else, like a call, for example.

Either way, you can now spend just 2 minutes booting up. This has now reduced lost time from 50 minutes a week or 200 minutes a month to 10 minutes a week or 40 minutes a month.

This is a huge difference. Changing the order in which you complete tasks can have a similar impact.

TIP - 4

The One Minute Rule

As its name says, it is a method based on the minimum unit of time. It was created in Japan and has been used in both professional and personal aspects.

Orientals understand that everything is a process and that the great achievements are the result of continuous efforts.

The minute rule says that you should start making a change in your life for just one minute. But remember, you must apply it every day.

It's simple: everything that can be done in 1 minute, must be done now. Many people have a tendency to procrastinate these small tasks, thinking: "I'll do it later". And many of these small tasks, which can be accomplished quickly, tend to accumulate throughout the day, becoming a snowball's routine, very complicated to deal with. How about trying to eliminate the problem as soon as it appears?

This applies to more specific tasks, such as your inbox. If possible, send that email in a few minutes, send it. If the e-mail response will only take a few minutes, answer it.

This rule states that we should always complete tasks immediately if they take less than a minute.

This removes them from our mind, which means that they are not hovering over us and causing stress.

TIP - 5

Rule 80/20

Pareto's Rule 80/20 was created by the Italian economist Vilfredo Pareto in the early 20th century. He shared this principle from observations and studies in several different areas that demonstrated a logic that 20% of our efforts are responsible for 80% of our results.

Rule 80/20 is widely used by organizations, both to solve internal problems and to evaluate the quality of products and improve processes as a whole. It also serves to decide which issues should be given priority and which can wait.

With this you can understand the importance of good time management, which is usually an untapped resource, which reduces productivity due to the lack of focus on what will really bring results. This way, if you focus your attention and your efforts on the most important 20%, be it in your business, focusing on 20% of the most profitable customers and products... Whether focusing on 20% of the most important tasks... Or on 20% of most important characteristics of your product ... Your Results will be better.

In short, to improve the outcome of what is being analyzed, it is necessary to focus on the issues that produce most of the desired results.

You must define your goals while paying attention to priorities. From that definition, prioritize those that need to be completed first, to those that will bring immediate results. Generally, 20% of the entire list of goals will have a high priority.

Now set your goals and deadlines for delivering them: as important as knowing the goals, is setting the goals. They must have a deadline for execution and delivery. In this phase of the work, productivity is guided by the organization. So don't waste your time.

Remember, do not waste time on activities that will not bring effective results: it is normal for activities that were not planned to occur throughout the day. You must identify whether the demand is urgent or not and prioritize those that will bring effective results.

Say "no" to tasks that are not your responsibility. This can be a difficult task, especially if it comes from a superior. But it is necessary to learn to say "no" so that there is no overload and mainly so that your goal is accomplished.

Save time: managing time is essential when you want to achieve the result without surprises. Asking or delegating help from colleagues to perform certain tasks can be instrumental in increasing your productivity. Rethink that!

At the end of the workday, analyze if you are managing to meet all your goals and deadlines, analyze if your productivity is increasing.

So the key word for productivity is prioritizing time. By applying Rule 80/20 to activities that will really make a difference, we will be on the path to success.

TIP - 6

Pomodoro

The Pomodoro technique was developed in the late 1980s by the Italian Francesco Cirillo, who was looking for a way to increase his productivity in studies. For this, he used a kitchen timer in the shape of a tomato (pomodoro, in Italian). This timer turned for 25 minutes, making a loud noise at the end of that period. In the meantime, Cirillo concentrated on his tasks without interruption, remaining 100% focused. Upon realizing the satisfactory results, he released his technique in 1992.

So with this technique, you will use stopwatches to control the time you should focus exclusively on work and when you will take a break.

First make a planning of the tasks, prioritize the items that should be done on the day. This allows you to estimate the tasks that require the most effort. As each pomodoro refers to a period of 25 minutes, which must be recorded in the list, it is possible to make a self-observation of how the time should be spent. Let's go to the Pomodoro walkthrough:

-List the tasks to be performed,

-Set the timer to the desired time (usually 25 minutes),

-Choose the initial task and work on this task until the alarm rings and in case any important distraction arises, a and return to focus immediately;

-Make an appointment at each pause, after the fourth appointment, take a longer break (10-30 minutes), resetting the appointment count and returning to the first step.

Planning, timing, and recording are fundamental to the technique. The goal of the technique is to reduce the time of interruptions, postponing other activities that interrupt Pomodoro.

The author of the technique encourages a low-tech approach, using only a stopwatch, pencil and paper. However, there are hundreds of software that assist in the application of this technique and do not require a kitchen timer.

TIP - 7

Rescue Time

Rescue Time is software to control your productivity while using your computer. This software has a free version that is usually sufficient for some types of users and has a PRO version, a version for Windows and another for Mac, which makes it possible to use it on almost all computers.

When Rescue Time is installed on your computer, it controls everything you do while working online or offline. It monitors all the pages you browse, how much time you dedicate to them, among many other things, generating statistical data so you can know where you spend the most time.

In addition to monitoring computer usage, this software also allows you to set goals, such as: "go an hour without accessing social networks", and apply different degrees of distraction to the different sites you browse and programs you use and tell you, according to statistics, what is your best day and time to work.

The important thing is to manage the use of your time, you can use other software, if it does not adapt to Rescue Time, such as: Timely, Toggl, Free Time and My Minutes for example.

In other words, knowing where your time is really going, you will have more control over how you spend that time.

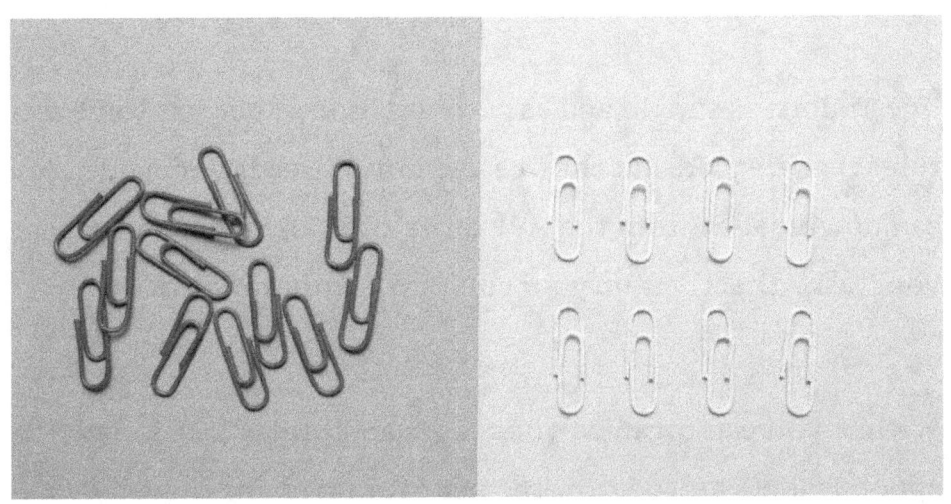

TIP - 8

Todoist

The Todoist is software to help you function in the organization in a simple way and practice. With it, you organize ideas, daily goals, future plans, start to have a vision of the whole and see your commitments more palpably, starting your day with an overview of everything that needs to be done.

The Todoist is simple and easy to use, is free, but has some features that are paid. But the free version is already very good. You can download it from the APP Store or Google Play or manage your tasks directly from your computer, from any browser.

With it you can organize your tasks and projects and view the appointments for today or the next 7, organizing them by date, priority etc. It is possible to organize your tasks as "delegated to me" or "delegated to other people", when they do not depend on you. In addition to organizing recurring tasks.

Nothing better than finishing all the tasks for the day, right? The application allows you to view completed tasks and you can relax, with the certainty that you have left nothing behind. And if you haven't been able to complete all the tasks for the day, don't worry. They do not disappear from the application, they just appear at the top as "overdue".

There are other software with similar functions, in case you want to try: Trello ; Evernote ; Microsoft One Note; OmniFocus ; Optmized ; Habit Bull; Habitica and Epic Win.

TIP - 9

SmartWatch

The smartwatches will change the way you work. That's right! If you believed that these devices would be useful only for entertainment, learn how this technology can be applied in the professional world.

On a day-to-day basis, you can time your meditation minutes

or keep track of your walk, run or bike . You can change your eating habits and even check the quality of your sleep. The smartwatches are an ideal fitness accessory for those who like to take care of health. This is a recurring feature for most users of these devices.

Now at work, all the information you need to access and the commands you need to give are at your fingertips, you won't need to take your phone out of your pocket or touch it.

It is enough that the device is connected, usually by bluetooth, to the smartphone to access its apps. Even away from the computer, you will not miss any notification, message, request or idea. The trend is that smartwatches increasingly resemble smartphones.

The smarthwatches are the next phase of the mobile revolution, but the key to the success of this technology is at work in applications. With the applications we can:

Measure the time invested by professionals in their tasks.

Better understand if the distribution of demands to employees is sensible or if there are bottlenecks.

Find out what motivates people the most and what should keep them engaged at work.

Access the priorities of the day, without having to resort to memory, an agenda or even the computer or cell phone screen.

Measure the time invested in the tasks, and deliver them with the same ease, in order to value your effort, and check if the hours contracted by the client are consistent.

Receive quick directions and answer emails from customers.

A smartwatch is a surprisingly powerful tool for productivity. In addition to allowing you to receive notifications on your wrist (meaning that your phone can stay securely in your pocket), you can add task items and more to your wrist, ensuring that they are always easily accessible, however, all of these possibilities of use, depend on the applications available, these applications will be crucial to dictate your success.

TIP - 10

Notion

Notion is a multifunctional organization application, completely free, with a web version and applications for both iOS and Android . In addition, there is a monthly subscription option for teams.

The Notion works basically as an organized and hierarchical system of blank sheets. Each "page" you create inside it appears on your screen as a note. In the side menu you can organize these notes the way you want, grouping with each other as needed.

Described by some as a "second brain", Notion is an extremely powerful note-taking application that allows you to create embedded web pages, tables, lists, images and videos and more.

It is extremely flexible, easy to use and can adapt to the way you want to use it.

There are other software with similar functions, if you want to try, like Evernote and Microsoft One Note.

TIP - 11

Freedom

Wasting less time on cell phones and social media has become a concern for many users. Smartphones are indispensable in everyday life, but also a problem for those who cannot let it aside. With constant notifications on the devices, it is possible to decrease productivity at work.

Freedom is an application for Android , iOS and computers that blocks applications that distract the user. Through login and password, the tool is able to create blocking sessions for pre-selected applications on different devices, preventing programs from connecting to the Internet. In addition, the service has a version for browsers on Mac OS and Windows, which facilitates the activation of restrictions without touching mobile devices.

The Freedom promises to limit access of applications easily. This is something powerful, for those who are easily distracted by social networks, while they must work!

TIP - 12

The Right Keyboard

In the digital age, much of what we consider 'productivity' happens on the computer. Being productive tends to mean writing emails, filling in data entry and writing texts.

Choosing the keyboard for your computer, tablet or other device is very important. The keyboard is an indispensable accessory for any computer user, the keyboard models can all look the same and this lack of knowledge often leads to this item not receiving the necessary attention at the time of purchase.

In addition to the brand and type of keyboard, it is recommended to pay attention to issues such as pattern, layout, configuration, functions, ease of installation, size, height adjustment, connection and power supply to make the right choice.

Today, with technological developments, keyboards are capable of much more. The extra buttons allow you to control different media, launch programs or applications, control volume and image settings. Some models have programmable buttons, where you can customize the commands for each key according to your needs.

There are wireless models that can be used remotely, eliminating the tangle of wires and allowing use at any distance and surface you desire and are still easy to transport.

However, for those who need high performance, such as gamers, typists and writers, mechanical keyboards are the best, as they are more resistant and quick to respond.

If you choose an imported model, check if the keyboard is compatible with the local standard as QWERTY, QWERTZ, AZERTY and layout adopted on your country. Non-standard keyboards can be more complicated to use.

Height adjustment is a very important factor for the comfort of using your keyboard and typing position. Fortunately, most models, even the simplest, have this type of regulation.

The durability of keys on a keyboard is a factor that depends directly on the material they are made of. In general, mechanical type keys are more durable.

And remember to research well, because it is possible to find models with characteristics from different groups on the market. Mechanical keyboards can be ergonomic, as well as ergonomic keyboards can be wireless, and so on.

The values of the keyboards will vary according to the make and model, but remember: not always the best and most complete is the most suitable for you. When choosing, consider your needs.

TIP - 13

Finger Positioning

Have you ever wondered if you are placing your hands correctly on the keyboard?

Arrange the keyboard so that it is tilted. This helps with typing and prevents possible hand injuries after hours of continuous use of the computer.

To start, don't put any fingers on the keyboard, but think about how they should position themselves. First, your fingers should form a U when they are placed on the keys.

Raise the handles slightly above the height of the table (if using a notebook). Thus, you will leave your fists at a healthier angle.

Learn a little about the names of the keyboard rows. The row in which the hands are placed is called the "main row". The rows directly above and below it are called "top row" and "bottom row", respectively. You should keep your hands in the main row until you are ready to press any key.

Place your left hand on the keyboard. Place your little finger on the A key, the ring on the S key, the middle finger on the D key and the index finger on the F key.

Place your right hand on the keyboard. Place your little finger on the L key, the ring finger on the K key, the middle finger on the J key and the index finger on the H key.

If the keyboard has a numeric keypad, you will need to move your hand to type the numbers or you can use the row on the alphanumeric keypad.

You should only remove your hands from the keyboard to press a function key. Keep them in place while typing.

The thumbs should be in the space bar of the keyboard. The left should be on the left side of the space bar and the right on the right side.

After a few weeks you won't even remember how you used the keyboard before. Over time, you will stop using inappropriate typing positions and avoid injury.

Let this be a guide, but not a basic rule, as you may find that it depends on the size of your hands and your keyboard.

TIP - 14

Dvorak

The Dvorak keyboard is considered more efficient than the QWERTY because the most common letters are in the home row: the vowels in the left hand and the most used consonants (DHTNS) in the right hand. This increases the parallelism between the hands and they also move much less to get to the next letter.

But it is necessary to adapt to the keyboard, it takes about a week to get used to the layout, then two more weeks to gain a minimum speed. During that time, it is a test of patience; you won't be able to type very fast and will need to take breaks frequently. On top of that you have to relearn all shortcuts like CTRL-C, CTRL-V, CTRL-S etc.

Some QWERTY users can switch to Dvorak. But if they don't want to change, they are also right, as it requires adaptation.

The Dvorak is an alternative keyboard layout which is supposed to be more efficient to write and that is very popular with some coders and writers. It will take a while to learn and the evidence is mixed, but if you find it easy to adapt, give it a try!

TIP - 15

Have A Plant

Your office is the space where you will do your work. It can make you more or less productive, so it is crucial to ensure that it stimulates your productivity.

A plant can have a big impact on the feel of an office, because it introduces something natural into the environment. In addition, this practice of growing plants is good for health, since the plant makes the air in the environment cleaner and more humid. Here are some benefits of having plants in the workplace:

-Happier environment.

-Filters the air.

-Increases the humidity of the air.

-Reduces stress.

-Increases productivity.

Check out some plants recommended for an office:

Cactus - It does not need to be watered frequently, as they can store much more water than other species.

Succulents - This species has plump leaves that reserve water. This characteristic makes it extremely easy to grow.

Jade plant - It belongs to the succulent family, so it is very resistant. By reversing water, it is much easier to care for and becomes a great option for an office.

Spyder Plant (Chlorophytum comosum) - This plant requires almost no maintenance and adapts very well in any environment, including those with air conditioning. Because it has thick roots, it also reserves a lot of water and still adapts to partial light.

Aloe Vera - This plant is also part of the succulent family, so it supports half shade and temperature variations.

Ivy - In the growth phase, this plant needs frequent watering, but when its size is established, it will require less watering and adapts very well indoors, including with air conditioning.

Snakeplant (Dracaena trifasciata) - They can easily survive low levels of light and watering, they are basically designed for office life.

Bamboo - In addition to giving your desk a Zen touch, bamboo needs very little light. As it is an aquatic plant, it needs water more frequently than the others. It is important to keep the roots always moist.

Plants not only decorate the environment, they give the feeling of life, tranquility and warmth. This calms us down, reassures us, and our minds are even more creative.

TIP - 16

Make It Inspiring

When you set up an Office at Home, for sure, functionality is the first thing that comes to mind, but you should also think about comfort and a way to make this environment more inspiring. See the tips below for your office:

Have a wall of inspiration. You can hang images that inspire you to work on a grid mural, a cork mural or in small comics, it is important that these images are in front of you while you work.

Try to leave your table by the window. Sometimes we are very focused on work, but we also need to rest our eyes and mind, placing the table near a window can be a solution, because then you can spend a few minutes looking at something other than the computer screen improving your inspiration, in addition to natural light being great, because it helps to keep the biological clock balanced. Those who do not have access to much external lighting can and should use suitable lamps.

Have plants. It doesn't matter the environment, but having plants around is always inspiring, in addition to improving air quality and calming us down.

Have fun and personal items. Make the space more fun, so that you can remember yourself, something relaxed and lively, to help you perform your tasks in a way not so tense.

Color! Some colors encourage creativity, such as orange, blue and green. How about painting your desk wall in one of those colors? It may be a good idea to make the environment more inspiring.

Available tools. Let your work tools in sight, regardless of their type of work, brushes, colored pens, staplers, spools of thread... Let all the shows, to make it easier to put their ideas into practice.

Have a comfortable chair. Nothing worse than sitting in an uncomfortable chair for hours. This causes you to lose focus on work and can even cause posture problems. Have a chair that you feel comfortable in, and that is part of that inspiring environment you are building.

Remember the organization. For some people, mess is part of the creation process, but when it lasts for a long time, it can cause stress and anxiety. So, remember to clean up your environment when you're done. This will make you much more willing to work well the next day.

Decorating your office with things that inspire you is a fantastic way to become more productive and creative. When we find work inspiring, it makes it inherently motivating, so your work will be much more enjoyable.

TIP - 17

Departmentalization

Home Office, is an environment in the home that has become proof of how our relationship with work has changed, and of course, is constantly evolving.

We always look for a little space inside the house to dedicate time to our work. Rooms, bedrooms and even balconies take on new meaning when we decide that part of our time there will be to focus on different projects. We must first decide where we will make our home office, taking into account that whatever your job, you will need to have tranquility and good lighting. If it is possible to guarantee natural lighting for your space, even better.

For those who live in houses with a good outdoor area, it is even possible to design an environment separate from everything else, creating your private haven when it comes to work. This helps in the search for silence and concentration, making you separate the home / work universes perfectly.

Apartment balconies can also become your office, be it the whole area or just a part, it all depends on your needs. However, it is not always possible to reserve a room especially for creating a home office. In this case, the most frequent option is to separate a space in the bedroom or living room.

Even so, to Departmentalize the workplace is necessary. You will need space for a table and a chair, keep only your professional activities nearby.

Shelf with books, pictures, a space for organizing post-its and even a different painting to "separate" the environment. Everything is valid when it comes to divide without the need for barriers, but always maintain common sense and prioritize the organization.

There are several options that can help you decorate the room while organizing it, such as memory boards and annual calendars. If your desk has drawers, organizing items such as trays, for example, can be used so that objects are not scattered. If the table does not have drawers, one option is to install shelves. Use pots or mugs to sector the materials as well. In addition, choose to leave only the essential materials for your work on the table. This way, you avoid many objects in sight that end up leaving the environment, in turn, more charged. Since, in some cases, this can influence even your productivity.

TIP - 18

Exercise

Many think that the benefits of physical exercise are only related to the results on the body and health. But physical activities also influence your job performance.

The sedentary has information processing more slowly, forgets things more often, and consequently feels frustrated. What makes you a less efficient person at work and makes living with your colleagues more difficult.

Consider the following benefits to your performance at work, when you include some physical activity in your routine:

-Greater concentration;

-Facilitates learning; Improves mental stamina;

-Helps in creativity;

-Decreases stress;

-Improves mood.

Despite so many physical, psychological and cognitive benefits, many people still see exercise as a luxury, something they would do only if they had more time. So it's time to consider exercise as part of your job.

Exercise is extremely important for those who work at home. It can reverse the damage caused by spending hours sitting, and it becomes even more pertinent if you have no commute, and no reason to get up and cross the room, as we usually do within a company.

Doing some form of cardio - like running, cycling or walking will help you strengthen your heart. This will also help to increase your calorie burn throughout the day to ensure that you do not gain unwanted weight. The important thing is to start something, identify a physical activity that you really enjoy and start!

TIP - 19

Protect Your Sleep

Remember to leave work and relax, when your office is at home, this separation can be a bit complicated, avoid confusing your work time with leisure time whenever possible.

Disconnect your computer and cell phone from work, it is much easier to resist the temptation to check if an answer to that email has already arrived or new information about that project if you are disconnected. This will do you enormous good.

Set up your workspace and turn everything off, this will make you understand that the day is over for today. Now take care to recharge your energy, so that you can return the next day feeling refreshed.

Plan an activity to do at the end of the day, if possible, leave the house and take a walk around the block, leave the house as if you were leaving work and then go home. Do a physical exercise session, meditate or call family members every day at the same time. This will help you disconnect your mind from work and prepare you to spend the early evening relaxing.

Who has never felt the effects of a bad night's sleep? Tiredness, irritability, decreased productivity and slow thinking are just some of the symptoms of sleep at work.

The quality of your sleep is very important, your work and your health can be compromised by sleeping badly. Remember to make sure you get enough sleep.

Here are some tips for a good sleep and to be happy at work:

-Sleep in a comfortable, dark, quiet and cool place.

-Have rituals before bed: prayer, meditation or a hot bath, for example.

-If you wake up early in the morning, don't look at your watch.

-Practice physical activities, preferably two hours before bed.

-Opt for light meals at night, as difficult digestion prevents sleep.

-Avoid light-emitting devices, such as cell phones, for at least half an hour before bed. They stimulate the release of cortisol and attenuate the sleep hormone melatonin, making sleep very difficult.

Adequate sleep is essential to maintain quality of life, achieve the best professional results and increase longevity.

TIP - 20

Spend Some Time Outdoors

Spending time outdoors is a way to ensure that you counter the negative effects of working at home and therefore increase your ability to focus.

It is not just today that we know the importance of sunbathing. The sun is a source of vitamin D. This vitamin helps to fix calcium in the bones, which is important for all of us at all ages.

Of course, we have to be careful with the sun, protect ourselves with sunscreen, even more at these times when the action of UVA and UVB rays are stronger and more harmful, but we don't need to be averse to it.

To reach the required daily amount, we only need 10 to 15 minutes in contact with the sun daily, with only one third of the body exposed, such as arms and legs. This will be enough for a good production of this vitamin D.

Spending time outdoors not only increases sleep (which helps us to work better as we have seen), but also increases vitamin D, which helps regulate important hormones in the body related to focus, energy and metabolism. Fresh air is just as important, while vegetation can really help to increase creativity.

TIP - 21

Manage Your Time

Finally, the time for those who work at home is their most precious asset. Nothing can replace that time ... Useful and precious time!

It doesn't matter how rich or poor you are. No matter how many things are on your to-do list, new tasks will arrive regularly twenty-four hours a day. Sometimes we would need twenty-four more to be able to complete our commitments ... But that is not possible, so we need to manage our time.

We need to understand that we cannot spend all those 24 hours a day working. We have to sleep a few hours, set aside time to eat and there is an occasional bath too ... Isn't that right?

Our families and friends demand some of our time. Relationships must be nurtured. So ... We can't afford to work so many hours a day.

As our working time is limited, this means that we must make the most of the hours we work. We cannot waste time on unimportant details or on tasks that other people can do.

E-mail account efficiency: everyone has multiple e-mail accounts. We use one account for this and another for that. Checking all email accounts more than once a day can be a time consuming and time consuming task. Try to centralize all emails in just one account like Gmail or Outlook, this way you can access them all in one place and you can still keep all your email addresses.

Organize schedules to help you prioritize your workday: A scheduled workday is an efficient workday. You will accomplish much more in much less time, if you know in advance and can quickly see which task is next on your list. I like visuals. A time table is a visual aid. It can help you allocate your time efficiently and productively!

Focus on results-producing activities: When you schedule your workday, you need to make sure that the tasks scheduled are the ones that will actually make your business grow and prosper. Do not waste your time, effort and energy on tasks that can be performed by others. But take time to check outsourcing. Manage your time, make records. You will be surprised at how much time you waste over the course of several days.

Now don't get me wrong. We all need downtime. We should all relax our minds and our bodies. We cannot be work and business all the time, but we can limit our unproductive or counterproductive activities.

Time is precious and time is limited. We need to make the best possible use of every minute of every day that we can.

Thank you!

ABOUT THE AUTHOR

Lilian Aveiro

Lilian Aveiro was born in São Paulo is an HR Manager, Writer and Founder of Blog Viva Plena.

Before entering the world of writing, Lilian worked in the administrative department of several companies, the last years being in home office , which opened the opportunity to improve her knowledge in the digital world.

After a successful career helping several companies, Lilian now helps other people to organize and improve their quality of life, through a healthier lifestyle, seeking self-knowledge and evolving a little more each day.

Lilian likes to run, care for her orchids, manage her blog and always finds time for coffee with friends.

www.blogvivaplena.com.br
Author Page Amazon:https://amzn.to/38IsM2U

Facebook - viva-plena

Instagram - @vivaplenaoficial and @lilianaveirooficial

BOOKS BY THIS AUTHOR

Emotion And Reaction

Emotion and Reaction Maximize your Emotional Intelligence to Achieve Success!

Do you know what Emotional Intelligence is?

It can help you achieve success, both in your personal and professional life!

Here are some advantages of developing Emotional Intelligence:

-Ability to quickly assess people's strengths and weaknesses;
-Ability to persuade;
-Become an admirable person;
-Command for respect;
-Develop leadership skills;
-Low impression of threat;
-Make more friends.

If you want to evolve, have inner peace, self-control, but you are lost and don't know where to start, you need to learn to master your emotions and not be dominated by them and you want to discover your best version. This book is for you!

Emotional Intelligence can always be developed. It is always possible to improve it. It's never too late or too early to start!

With some simple techniques and daily practices, you will be able to balance your reason and your emotions, you will be able to control your life. You will know how to control your reaction to emotions! Becoming a successful person at work and in personal life!

Developing your Emotional Intelligence is the path to success!

Home Office + Productive

Working from home can be wonderful or extremely stressful!

The Home Office has been around for some time, but with the start of the pandemic, even those who have never considered working in this way, need to adapt. And the advantages are so many that many companies intend to maintain this model of work even after the end of the pandemic.

Most people complain about the lack of time they have for their daily activities due to the huge load of tasks they have to perform.

This book is for you who want to maintain your routine productive and efficient in the Home Office, but without neglecting your personal life and well-being.

With objective, practical and effective tips that will help you improve your job performance and quality of life. After all, Organization and Time Management are the keys to the balance between professional and personal life.

Emoção E Reação

Maximize sua Inteligência Emocional para Atingir o Sucesso!

Você sabe o que é Inteligência Emocional?

Ela poderá lhe ajudar a alcançar o sucesso, tanto na vida pessoal como profissional!

Veja algumas vantagens de se desenvolver a Inteligência Emocional:

-Capacidade de avaliar os pontos fortes e fracos das pessoas rapidamente;
-Capacidade de persuadir;
-Tornar-se uma pessoa admirável;
-Comandar pelo respeito;
-Desenvolver a capacidade de liderança;
-Baixa da impressão de ameaça;
-Fazer mais amigos.

Se você deseja evoluir, ter paz interior, autocontrole, mas está perdido e não sabe por onde começar, precisa aprender a dominar suas emoções e não ser dominado por elas e quer descobrir a sua melhor versão. Este livro é para você!

A Inteligência Emocional sempre pode ser desenvolvida. É sempre possível aprimorá-la. Nunca é tarde ou cedo para começar!

Com algumas técnicas simples e práticas diárias, você será capaz de equilibrar sua razão e suas emoções, será capaz de controlar sua vida. Saberá controlar sua reação às emoções! Tornando-se uma pessoa de sucesso no trabalho e na vida pessoal!

Desenvolver sua Inteligência Emocional é o caminho para o sucesso!

Home Office + Produtivo

Trabalhar em casa pode ser maravilhoso ou extremamente estressante!

O Home Office já existe há algum tempo, mas com o inicio da pandemia, mesmo quem nunca cogitou trabalhar desta forma, precisa se adaptar. E as vantagens são tantas que muitas empresas pretendem manter este modelo de trabalho mesmo após o fim da pandemia.

A maioria das pessoas reclama da falta de tempo que dispõe para suas atividades diárias devido à enorme carga de tarefas que tem para executar.

Este livro é para você que deseja manter uma rotina produtiva e eficiente no Home Office, mas sem descuidar da sua vida pessoal e do seu bem estar.

Com dicas objetivas, práticas e eficazes que lhe ajudarão a melhorar seu desempenho no trabalho e sua qualidade de vida. Afinal, Organização e Gerenciamento do tempo, são as chaves para o equilíbrio entre vida profissional e pessoal.

www.ingramcontent.com/pod-product-compliance
Lightning Source LLC
Chambersburg PA
CBHW071420210526
45465CB00001B/464